The Ultimate Beginner

BLUES GUITAR BASICS

Revised Edition

CONTENTS

Section 1: **The Basics**..2
    Reading Rhythm Notation...2
    Reading Tablature (TAB) and Fretboard Diagrams............3
    Reading Music Notation..4
Section 2: **Rhythm Guitar**..5
    Triplets and the Eighth-Note Shuffle................................5
    The 12-Bar Blues Progression...7
    Blues in the Key of A...7
    Other Rhythm Patterns..8
Section 3: **Blues Soloing**..12
    The Minor Pentatonic and Blues Scales...........................12
    Blues Phrasing...15
    Call and Response Phrasing..17
    Soloing Over the 12-Bar Progression...............................22
    Time to Play with the Band...24
Section 4: **The Slow Blues**...26
    The Quick Change...26
Section 5: **New Blues Scale Positions**.................................32
    Sweet Notes..34
    The B.B. King Secret Scale Pattern..................................35
    Vibrato..36
    Dynamics...36
    Matching Solos to Chords...39
Guitar TAB Glossary 47

An enhanced CD is included with the book to make learning easier and more enjoyable. The audio tracks are accessible with any CD player. Put the disc in your Mac or Windows computer to access the Tone-N-Tempo Changer software that lets you adjust the speed and pitch of the audio tracks. Track 1 on the CD is an introduction, and track 2 will help you get your guitar in tune.

Introduction
Track 1

Tuning Notes
Track 2

Keith Wyatt

Alfred Music
P.O. Box 10003
Van Nuys, CA 91410-0003
alfred.com

ISBN-10: 0-7390-8200-0 (Book & CD)
ISBN-13: 978-0-7390-8200-3 (Book & CD)

ISBN-10: 0-7390-8207-8 (Book, CD & DVD)
ISBN-13: 978-0-7390-8207-2 (Book, CD & DVD)

ISBN-10: 0-7579-0814-4 (DVD)
ISBN-13: 978-0-7579-0814-9 (DVD)

Cover photographs:
Guitar courtesy of Gibson USA.
Blue energy © iStockphoto.com / Raycat

Section One: The Basics

READING RHYTHM NOTATION

At the beginning of every song is a time signature. $\frac{4}{4}$ is the most common time signature:

$$\frac{4}{4}$$ = FOUR COUNTS TO A MEASURE
= A QUARTER NOTE RECEIVES ONE COUNT

The top number tells you how many counts per measure.
The bottom number tells you which kind of note receives one count.

The time value of a note is determined by three things:

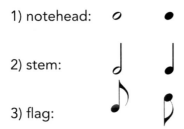

1) notehead:

2) stem:

3) flag:

O This is a whole note. The notehead is open and has no stem. In $\frac{4}{4}$ time, a whole note receives 4 counts.

This is a half note. It has an open notehead and a stem. A half note receives two counts.

This is a quarter note. It has a solid notehead and a stem. A quarter note receives one count.

This is an eighth note. It has a solid notehead and a stem with a flag attached. An eighth note receives one half count. Notice the counting includes "ands" (&) to show the half beats.

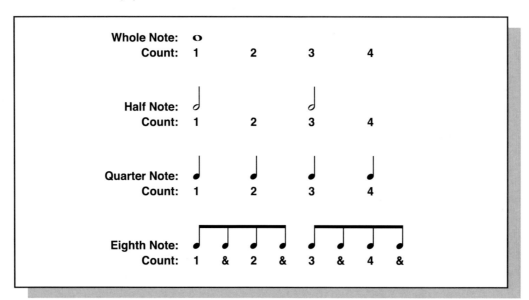

Whole Note:	**O**			
Count:	1	2	3	4
Half Note:				
Count:	1	2	3	4
Quarter Note:				
Count:	1	2	3	4
Eighth Note:				
Count:	1 & 2 &	3 & 4 &

Rests indicate silence, and there is a rest that corresponds to each note value. A whole rest ▬ lasts four beats, a half rest ▬ lasts two beats, a quarter rest 𝄽 lasts one beat, and an eighth note rest 𝄾 lasts one half count.

READING TABLATURE (TAB) AND FRETBOARD DIAGRAMS

Tablature (TAB) illustrates the location of notes on the neck of the guitar. This illustration compares the six strings of a guitar to the six lines of tablature.

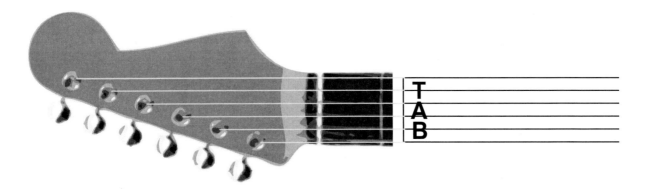

Notes are indicated by placing fret numbers on the strings. An "0" indicates an open string.

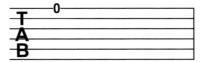

This tablature indicates to play the open, 1st, and 3rd frets on the 1st string.

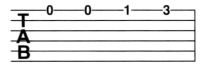

Tablature is usually used in conjunction with standard music notation. The rhythms and note names are indicated by the standard notation and the location of those notes on the guitar neck is indicated by the tablature.

Chords are often indicated in *chord block diagrams*. The vertical lines represent the strings and the horizontal lines represent the frets. Scales are often indicated with guitar *fretboard diagrams*. Here the strings are horizontal and the frets are vertical.

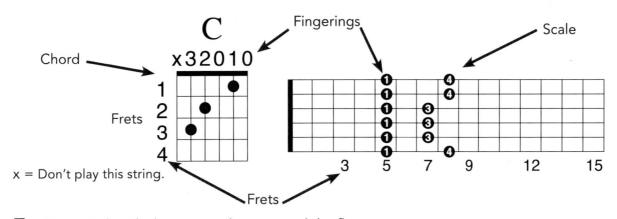

$\sqcap$ = *Downstroke*. Pluck or strum down toward the floor.

$\lor$ = *Upstroke*. Pluck or strum up toward the ceiling.

READING MUSIC NOTATION

Music is written on a *staff*. The staff consists of five lines and four spaces between the lines:

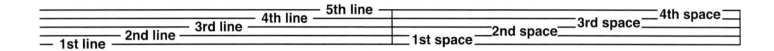

The names of the notes are the same as the first seven letters of the alphabet: A B C D E F G.

The notes are written in alphabetical order. The first (lowest) line is "E":

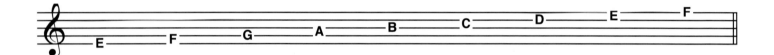

Notes can extend above and below the staff. When they do, *ledger lines* are added. Here is the approximate range of the guitar from the lowest note, open 6th-string "E," to a "B" on the 1st string at the 17th fret.

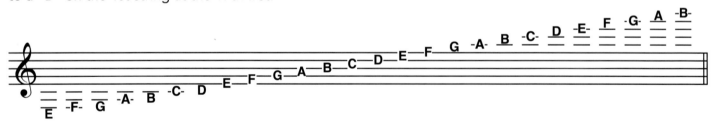

The staff is divided into *measures* by *bar lines*. A heavy double bar line marks the end of the music.

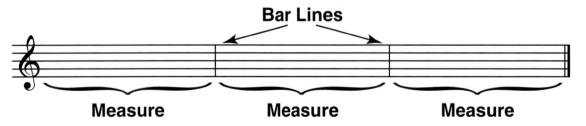

Section Two: Rhythm Guitar

TRIPLETS AND THE EIGHTH-NOTE SHUFFLE

Rhythm is the driving force behind the blues. It may not take many notes to play good blues, but the rhythm must be strongly felt. The *eighth-note triplet* is the most common rhythm in blues music. The eighth-note triplet divides a beat (one quarter note) into three equal parts. The *shuffle rhythm* uses the first and last notes of the triplet to create a smooth and relaxed feeling.

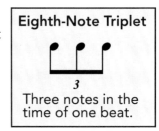

Example 1

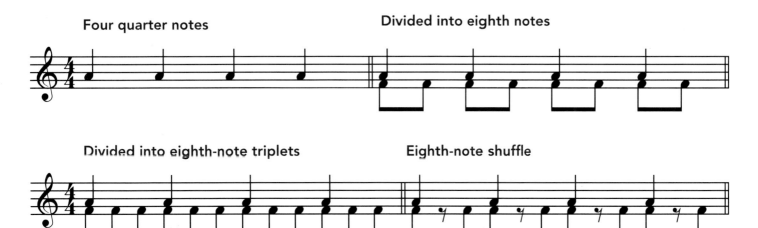

 **Example 2**
Track 2

 **Example 3**
Track 3

Accenting (>) the first note of each triplet figure brings out the natural, swinging quality of the shuffle. Let's also add *palm muting* (P.M., lay the pinky side of your picking hand across the strings directly next to the bridge to slightly mute the sound) with the picking hand by deadening the low E string. This makes for a percussive effect. Use only down-strokes.

Two- and three-note *chords* (notes played together) are made by harmonizing the E-note with notes on the A and D strings. This chord is known as E5 or an E *power chord.* Notice the *barre* symbol ⌒ in the three-note E5 chord diagram. This means to hold down two or more strings with one finger.

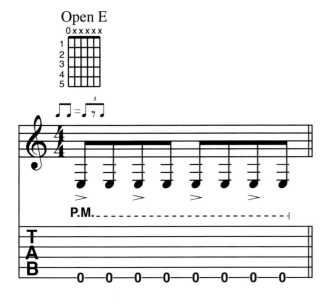

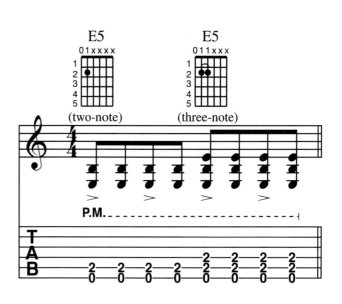

EXAMPLE 4

Track 4

Adding another chord (E6) helps us to play the main staple of blues guitar rhythms known as the **boogie**. Continue to accent and palm mute. Note the up-stroke on the last chord of the bar.

> ♯ = **Sharp**. A sharp means to play a note one **half step** (one fret) higher than it's **natural** (normal) position.
>
> * = **Key signature**. Indicates the notes on these lines and spaces are sharp throughout, unless marked with a natural sign ♮. In this example, the key signature has F♯, C♯, and G♯.

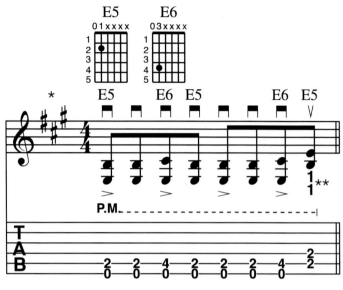

** Fingering. Barre with 1st finger

EXAMPLE 5

Track 5

If you move these "shapes" (E5 and E6) to the next two sets of strings you get A5 and A6 (on the 4th and 5th strings) and D5 and D6 (on the 3rd and 4th strings). These are all the chords needed for a typical 12-bar blues boogie pattern in the **key of A** (F♯, C♯, and G♯ in the key signature).

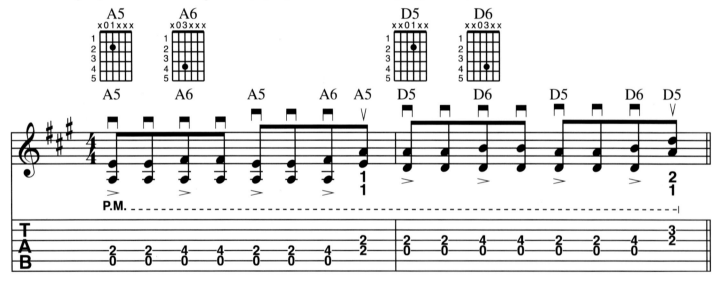

EXAMPLE 6

Track 6

In order to play in other keys, we must transform these open position chords into moveable barre chords. When played in 5th **position** (off the 5th fret), the A5, A6, D5, and D6 chords all sound identical to the open position versions, only now with new fingerings. The E5 and E6 end up being an octave higher than the originals.

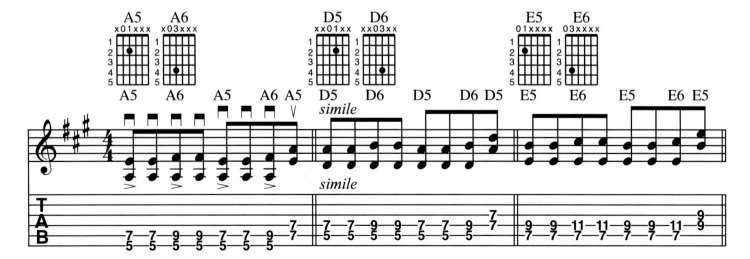

THE 12-BAR BLUES PROGRESSION

The *12-bar blues* is the most common form of the blues *progression* (series of chords). It is 12 measures long and uses the 1st, 4th, and 5th chords of the key. Those chords are usually indicated with Roman numerals (I, IV, and V) and can easily be determined by counting up through the alphabet from the key note. For example:

BLUES IN THE KEY OF A

A	B	C♯	D	E	F♯	G♯
I			IV	V		

THE A BLUES PROGRESSION

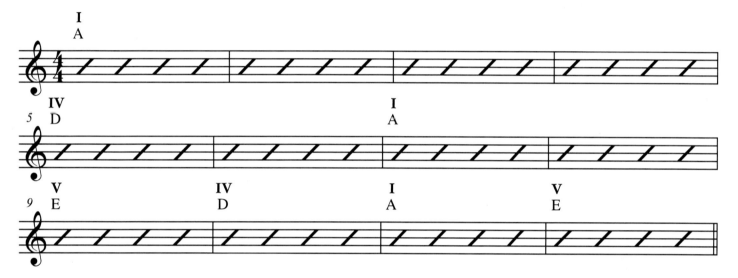

 **EXAMPLE 7**
Track 7

A common variation for the end of the progression is called a **turnaround** and it requires a new chord called E9. A turnaround marks the end of the progression and sets us up to repeat from the top. Notice how this last bar (bar 12) remains on the I chord for the first beat before an F9 is played on beat two, serving as a **passing chord** (a chord that does not fit in the key but leads to one that does) to E9, which hits on the "and" (&) of beat two.

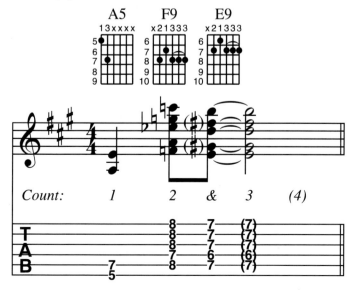

> ♭ = **Flat**. A flat means to play a note one half step lower than its natural position.

> ♮ = **Natural**. A natural indicates a note is neither sharp nor flat.

OTHER RHYTHM PATTERNS

Now that the fundamental rhythm pattern has been established, it is important to compliment it with contrasting patterns that can be played simultaneously or separately.

 **EXAMPLE 8**
Track 8

This first variation uses an A7 barre chord played with accented "stabs" on "1" and the "and" of 2. Notice there are only two stabs per measure, while the rest of the strums are muted string hits (✕) that serve as your **metronome** (a device that measures the speed of music and provides a steady beat to play with).

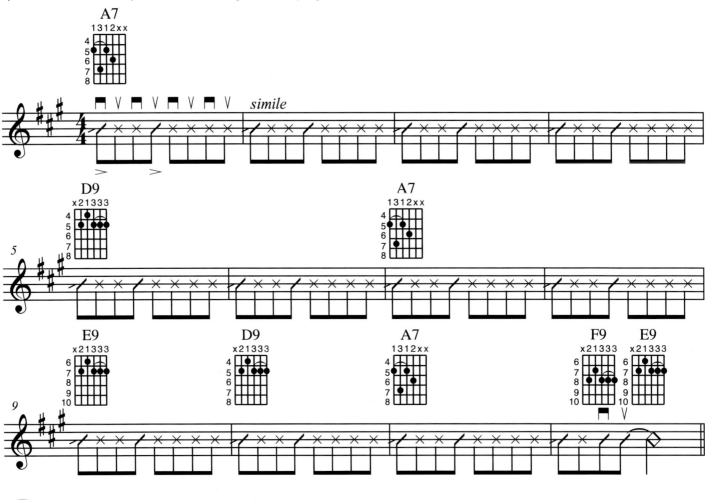

 **EXAMPLE 9**
Track 9

This variation involves a **hammer-on** while other notes are sustained. Barre the 1st finger across the top four strings at the 5th fret and strike the 2nd and 3rd strings. Hammer the 2nd finger onto the 3rd string/6th fret, thus sounding the note on the 6th fret without plucking; that is the hammer-on. A small 3rd-finger barre at the 7th fret is played before repeating the hammer-on. This idea is then transposed to the IV and V chords.

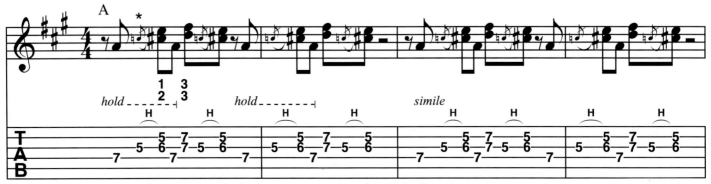

* This is a **grace note**, which is a quick, decorative note played right before the main note.

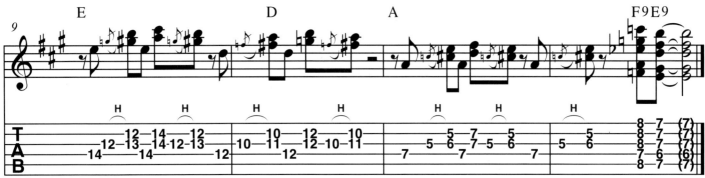

 **EXAMPLE 10**

Track 10

An alternative to hammering is *sliding* ╱. Move your fingers along the string after plucking to create a gliding sound. In this example, we slide into the I, IV, and V chords from a half step (one fret) below.

SL = Slide

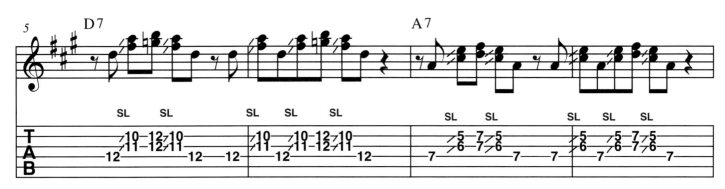

EXAMPLE II
Track 11

This example requires some quick changes of position and fingerings as it goes from
5th position to 7th position and back again. The chord at the 7th position is a two-note
voicing for A7—a useful sound for blues.

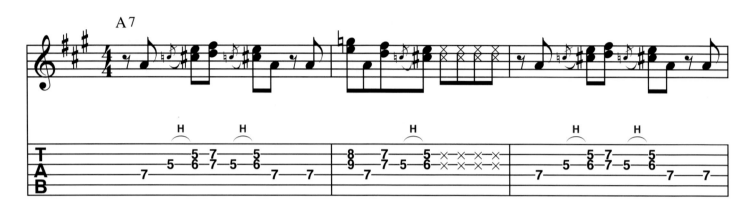

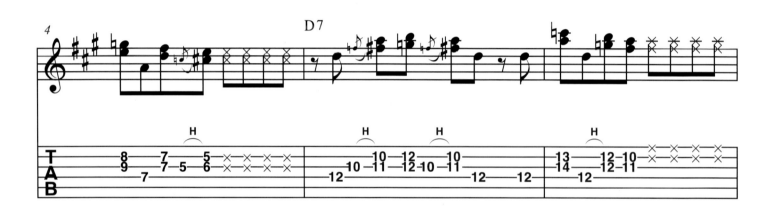

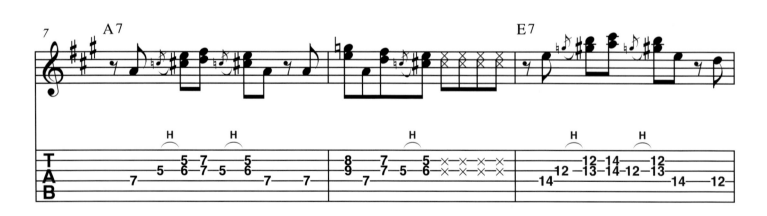

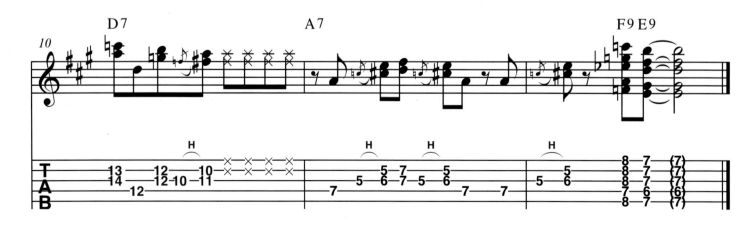

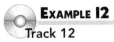

EXAMPLE 12

Track 12

With this variation, let's add the 1st string to the two-note chords of the last example. Notice how adding the high notes gives the chords more melodic interest. This pattern employs the hammer-on and the slide together.

Section Three: Blues Soloing

THE MINOR PENTATONIC AND BLUES SCALES

The most important sound for blues guitar is the **minor pentatonic scale**. This is a five-note scale derived from the full seven-note minor scale. In the key of A, the minor pentatonic scale is:

A   C   D   E   G

1   ♭3   4   5   ♭7

These minor pentatonic scales can be fingered across the neck in every position and octave, but we will concentrate on the most common fingerings used by blues guitarists.

EXAMPLE 13: THE A MINOR PENTATONIC SCALE
Track 13

This is the most common fingering for the minor pentatonic scale. It is shown here in the 5th position (key of A).

EXAMPLE 14: THE A BLUES SCALE
Track 14

Adding the note known as the ♭5 (E♭ in the key of A) makes the minor pentatonic scale even "bluesier." Now we have a six-note scale with this "blue note" added in two places. It is known as the **blues scale**.

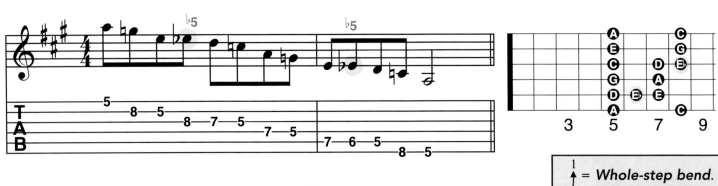

EXAMPLE 15
Track 15

The next example of blues phrasing uses the ♭5 to add "color" to the minor pentatonic scale. Notice how slurring (hammer-ons, pull-offs, and slides) gives the E♭ blue note a "singing" quality. Note the bend at the end of the first line.

↑ = **Whole-step bend**. Push the string up or pull it down to create a gliding sound up to a note one whole step (two frets) higher. See page 47 for more on bending techniques.

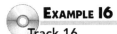

EXAMPLE 16

Track 16

Here is another example that highlights the ♭5 in the blues scale.

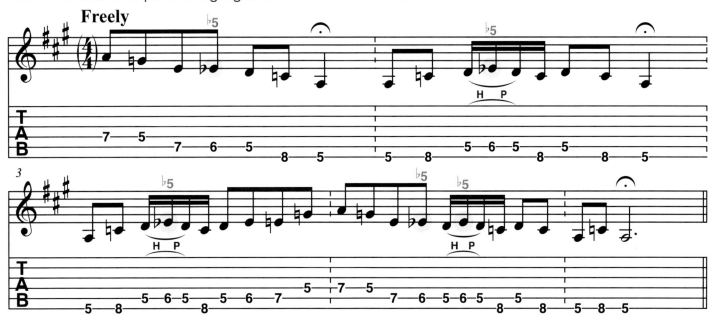

EXAMPLE 17

To get your fingers used to the blues scale pattern, try running up and down this complete 5th position version of the blues scale.

EXAMPLE 18
Track 17

Now we will extend the scale fingering. This will give you more room to move around the neck while improvising. These extensions are affectionately known as "boxes" to guitar players. The lower extension (or blues "box") adds a low G and a C, which sounds exactly the same as the C you've been playing on the 6th string, 8th fret. The high extension adds an alternate fingering for the E and A and a new high C and D.

Your 1st and 3rd fingers create the "boxes" as you shift in and out of 5th position.

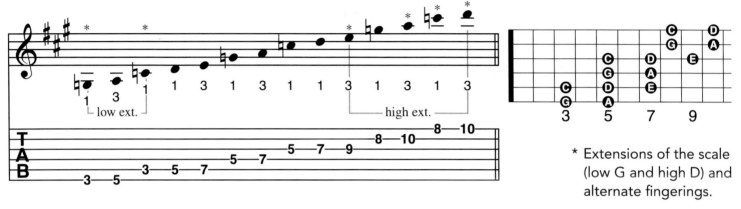

* Extensions of the scale (low G and high D) and alternate fingerings.

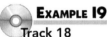

EXAMPLE 19
Track 18

The high extension is a hot spot in blues guitar playing. All five notes of the minor pentatonic scale are found here, and it's a great place to bend notes. This next example shows some blues phrases with bends on the 1st string. The bend to E♭ is from the 10th fret (D). This type of bend is called a **ghost** or **pre-bend**. This is when you bend the string to the desired pitch before striking it. A **quarter-step bend** is used on the C note. This bend places the pitch between the note your finger is on and the note one half-step above (one fret).

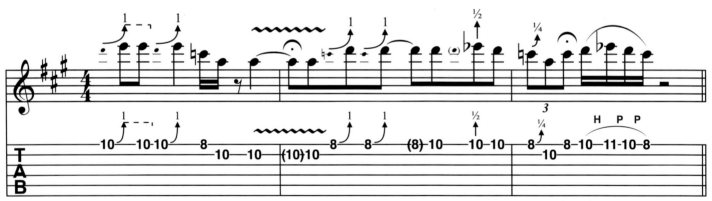

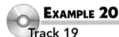

EXAMPLE 20
Track 19

Here is a three-octave blues scale pattern. This one again highlights the ♭5.

BLUES PHRASING

Everything we have played so far has been built from the same six notes: A, C, D, E♭, E, and G. What you do with them in terms of note choice and rhythm is known as *phrasing*. The more you play the guitar as if you were singing, the more musical you will be. When you sing, you tend to use only what is musically important, as opposed to just singing scales. Breathing when you sing is equivalent to resting. Not playing (or resting) when you are soloing can be as important as playing.

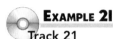

EXAMPLE 21
Track 21

This short phrase proves that "less is more." Built into this lick is a beginning (the first five notes), a middle (the rest), and an ending (from E♭ to the last A). The melody of these notes is memorable and easy to sing, while the rhythm feels very natural in the way it fits the shuffle groove.

EXAMPLE 22
Track 22

Employing hammer-ons and *pull-offs* (raising the upper finger off a higher note to sound the lower note being held by the lower finger) connects or slurs the notes together smoothly—creating a more "vocal" sound.

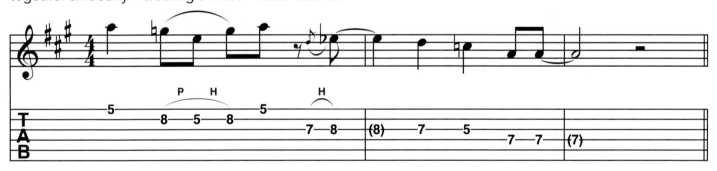

EXAMPLE 23
Track 23

Adding slides is another way of imitating the voice. The first slide takes you to A on the 10th fret. The second slide replaces the hammer-on from the grace note D.

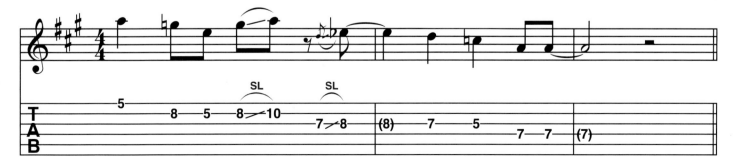

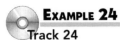

EXAMPLE 24
Track 24

The last technique we will add is the bend. In this case, a quarter-step bend is used on the G and C notes. Next is a half-step bend from D to E♭ (the ♭5).

EXAMPLE 25: A BLUES SCALE BENDS
Track 25

This example illustrates the most common bends in the blues scale. The first is from the ♭7 (G) up to A on the 2nd string. The next bend is also from D on the 3rd string, but this time up a half-step to E♭.

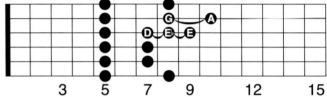

EXAMPLE 26
Track 26

Practically every guitar player who plays blues makes use of the ¼ step bend. It is usually heard with the ♭3rd. This example covers three different octaves of the ♭3 (C) in the key of A.

CALL AND RESPONSE PHRASING

Before the proliferation of guitar TAB books and instructional videos, blues musicians taught each other simply by listening and copying what they heard. It still remains the best way to learn music, because it helps you discover how to listen and interpret what you hear.

 **EXAMPLE 27**
Track 27

In this example I'll play a two-bar phrase—that is the **call**. Your **response** will be to try to copy what you hear on the spot. Don't get frustrated if you can't pick up each lick perfectly at first. This takes a lot of practice. The most important thing is to get as close to the "vibe" and the general feeling of a particular phrase. Try this with the recording a few times before checking out the transcription below.

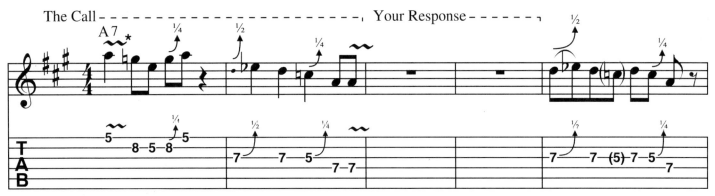

* **Vibrato**. A wavering or fluctuation of pitch, usually rapid, used for an expressive, vocal effect. Covered in detail on page 36.

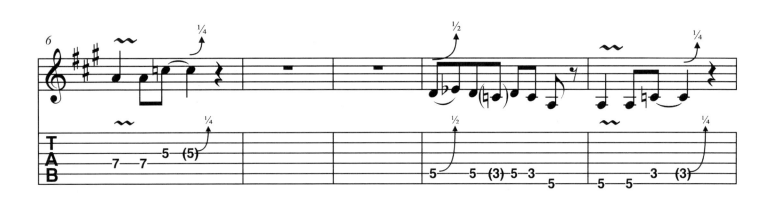

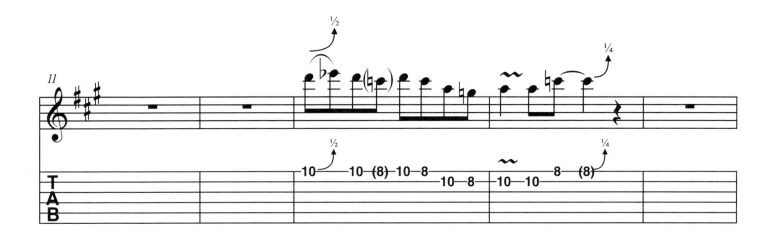

* A small dot above a note is called **staccato** and means to play the note shorter than its value.

SOLOING OVER THE 12-BAR PROGRESSION

The short phrases we have been learning can be "plugged in" to any 12-bar blues solo. As you know, the magic of the blues scale is that you can use it over all three chords in the progression. Here are some approaches for soloing over the 12-bar progression that include call and response, phrasing like a blues singer, and working the turnaround to the V chord at the end of the progression into your solo.

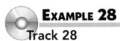 **EXAMPLE 28**
Track 28

You can literally play the same lick over each chord in the blues progression. It is balanced, makes sense, and it feels good. Here is a blues scale lick played over the entire progression.

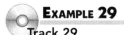

Example 29
Track 29

Traditionally, blues singers use three phrases in a 12-bar blues: the call over the I chord, the same call again (perhaps with slight variation) over the IV chord, and then a different, contrasting response over the V chord. This example demonstrates how it can be done with a guitar instead. The first eight bars are the same as the previous example, so only the V chord response (the last four bars) is shown here.

Bars 9–12

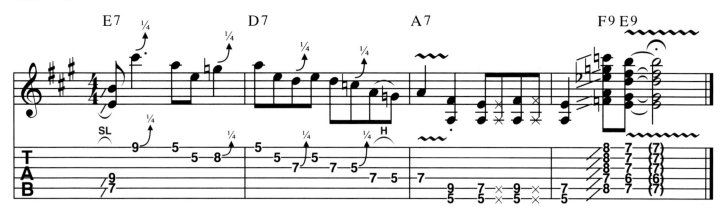

Example 30
Track 30

A staple of good blues soloing is to acknowledge the V chord turnaround at the end of the progression by working the root of the chord (in this case, E) into your line. When the rhythm section hits the V chord in bar 12, end your phrase with an E note. This turnaround lick uses the 5th-string, 7th-fret E to end the phrase. Again, I've only indicated the last four bars.

Bars 9–12

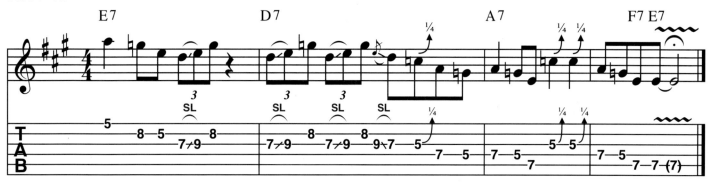

TIME TO PLAY WITH THE BAND

Following is a three-chorus blues solo that demonstrates how to bring the elements we have been working on together into a solid, well-paced solo. At the end of the solo, we'll start the rhythm section from the top so you can play along.

About Soloing

Think of a solo as a big phrase; it should have a beginning, a middle, and an ending. It's a good idea to pace your solo so that not too much happens too soon. Use all the material we have covered and consider taking it up an octave to 17th position, where the blues scale pattern repeats. Remember, it doesn't take a whole lot of positions and notes to play the blues—some of the greatest blues guitarists of all time have used scarcely more than two or three positions.

EXAMPLE 31
Track 31

Section Four: The Slow Blues

A *slow blues* can be thought of as a slowed down shuffle. Remember, in a shuffle each quarter note beat is subdivided into a triplet with the first and last note of the triplet being accented.

In a slow blues, you feel all three notes of each triplet. Count off the four triplets in the bar as:

1	2	3	**4**	5	6	7	8	9	**10**	11	12

Accent the 4th and 10th notes in the bar and those become the **backbeats**. This is known as $\frac{12}{8}$ meter: 12 beats per measure, and an eighth note gets one beat.

THE QUICK CHANGE

Until now, the 12-bar progression remained on the I chord for the opening four bars. A common variation is the quick change to the IV chord in bar 2. We return to the I chord for bars 3 and 4, and the rest of the progression is unchanged. This is a traditional variation, and is usually talked about before a tune begins.

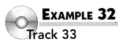

EXAMPLE 32
Track 33

Let's learn a rhythm pattern to help warm up to the quick change. This type of pattern originated with the great T-Bone Walker, the father of electric blues guitar. He was heavily involved with horn sections in his music, and this rhythm part attempts to imitate one. We will now be playing in the key of G. Everything we have been playing in A can easily be shifted down two frets to G. Here are the first four bars of a 12-bar blues in G with the quick change.

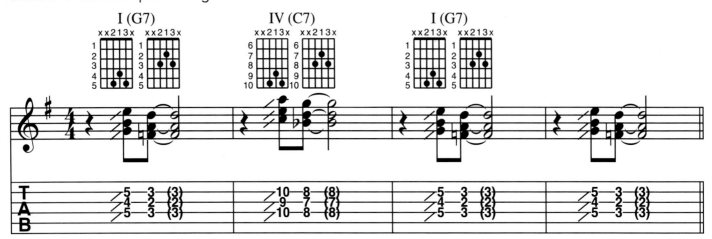

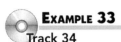

EXAMPLE 33
Track 34

The first of the two chord shapes found in the next example is derived from the familiar G major barre form at the 3rd fret. Delete the 6th and 5th strings and you're left with a major chord shape on the top four strings. Raising the 5th (D) of the chord a whole step up to E on the 2nd string gives us a G6 chord. The high G on the 1st string, 3rd fret tends to be optional. Shifting the shape down a whole step makes a G9 chord. The two sounds together are thought of as a substitute for the I chord (G7). When transposed to the IV and V chords, you now have all the substitute chord forms with which to play a 12-bar blues. The pattern always begins on the 2nd beat of the measure. Note the familiar turnaround at the end.

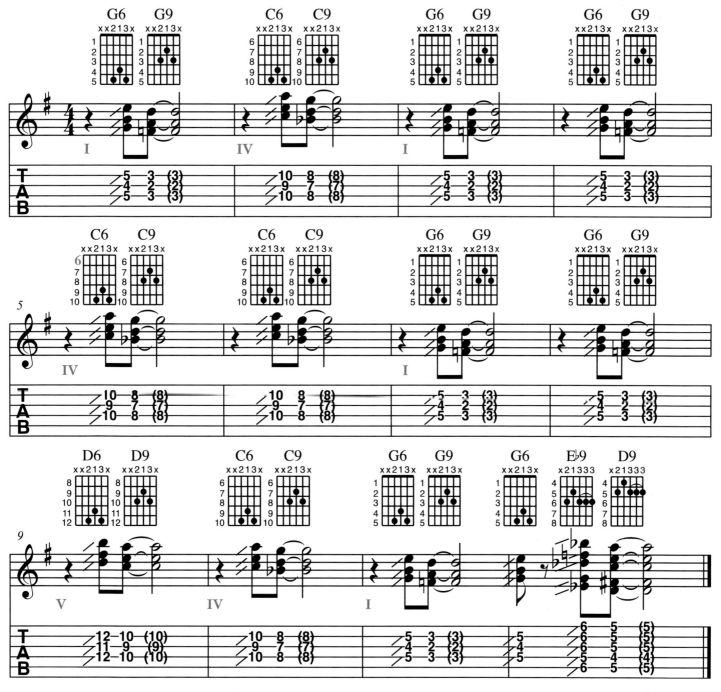

EXAMPLE 34

Track 35

There is often more than one place to play a particular chord on the guitar. Instead of moving high up the neck to play the IV and V chords, we can play them on the top three strings. This is a good way to limit your hand movement. Here we simply show the new shapes. Carry on through the entire progression as usual.

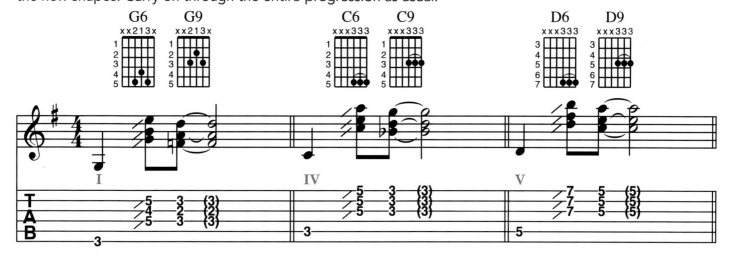

EXAMPLE 35
Track 36

Now let's add the optional 1st-string G to the G6 chord for another horn-section-inspired rhythm part. We're also going to use the 9th chord. Notice that all these shapes are approached by sliding from a half step below. This gives it some "grease."

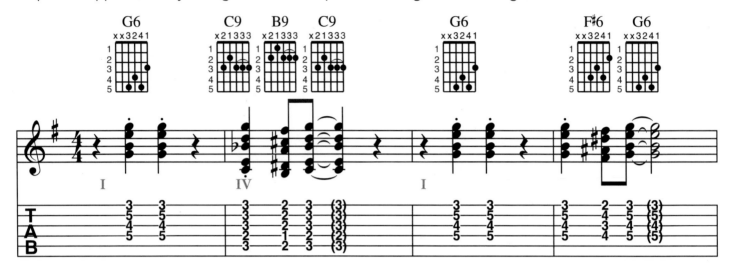

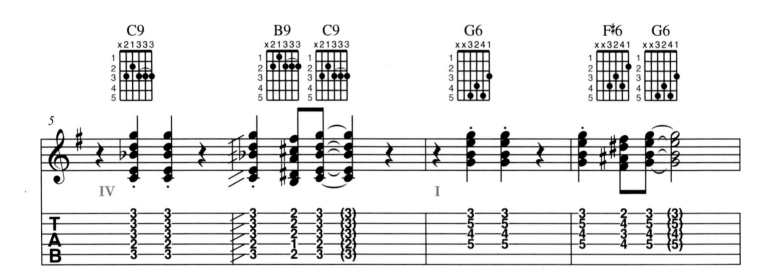

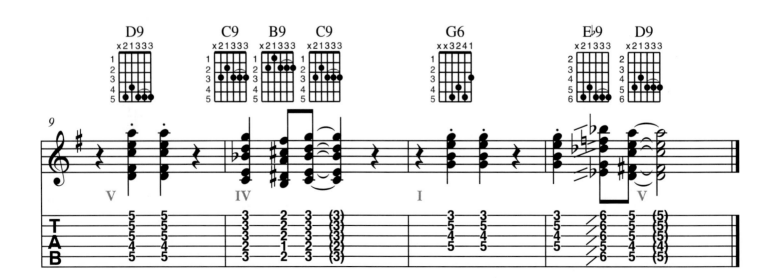

EXAMPLE 36: BLUES INTRO
Track 37

The last four bars of the blues progression can be used as an introduction as shown in this example.

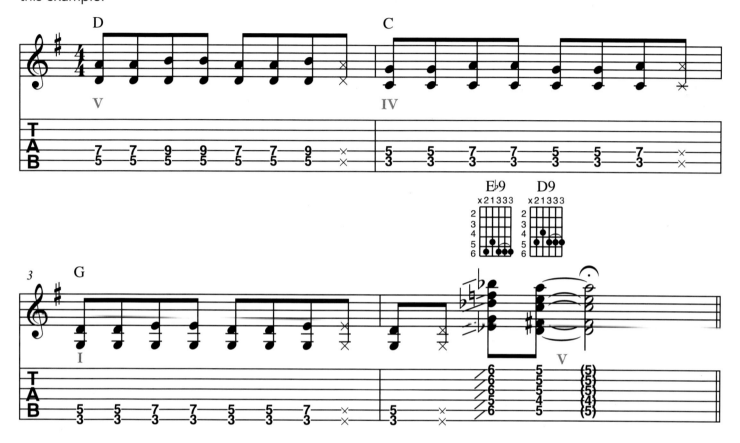

 EXAMPLE 37: BLUES ENDING
Track 38

At the end of a song, you'll want to finish on the I chord, in the same rhythmic place (beat two) of the 12th bar that you played the V chord turnaround. The V chord turnaround leads you back to the beginning. Playing the I chord at the end of the phrase sounds final.

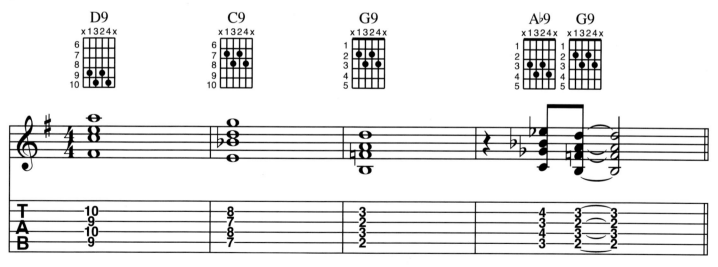

EXAMPLE 38
Track 39

This next example uses all of the techniques you've learned so far. It's a 12-bar blues, in the key of G (F♯ in the key siganture), with the intro from the V, to a quick change and a stop on I at the end. A space is left for the lead guitar to make a final statement.

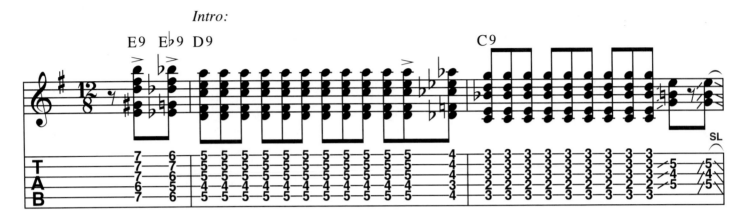

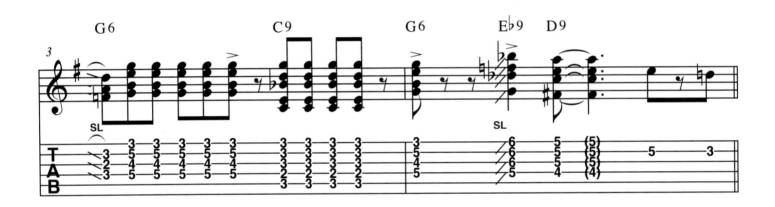

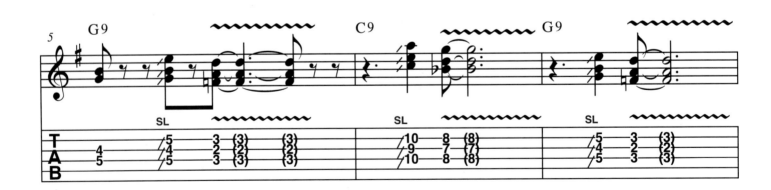

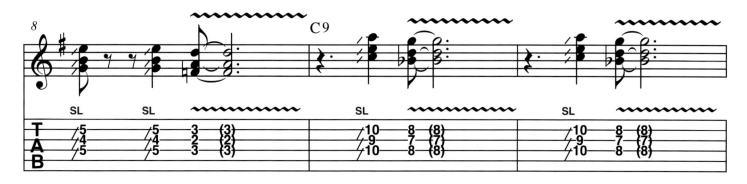

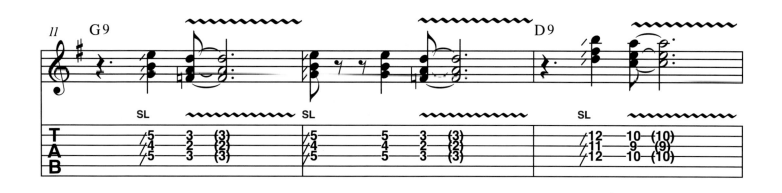

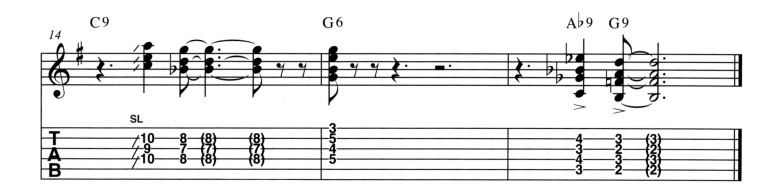

Section Five: New Blues Scale Positions

Let's quickly review the blues scale positions we learned in the key of A and transpose them to the key of G. The basic fingering for the G blues scale will lie in the 3rd position centering around the G barre chord with the low and high extensions then added. You can also jump up the neck an octave to where these patterns begin again, at the 15th position.

EXAMPLE 39
Track 40

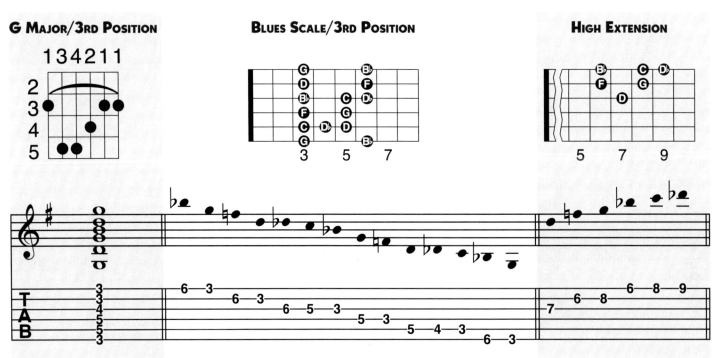

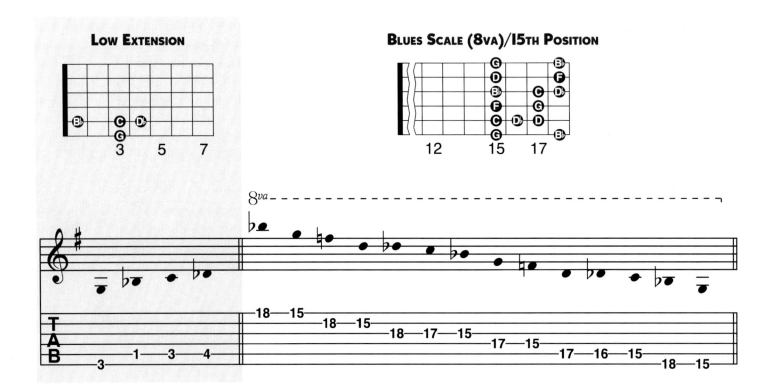

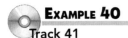

EXAMPLE 40
Track 41

It is very important to understand how scales are related to chords. The previous blues scale pattern was based around the G barre chord in 3rd position, and this new pattern is centered around the G barre chord in 10th position.

EXAMPLE 41
Track 42

Now let's add the remaining notes, including a low extension.

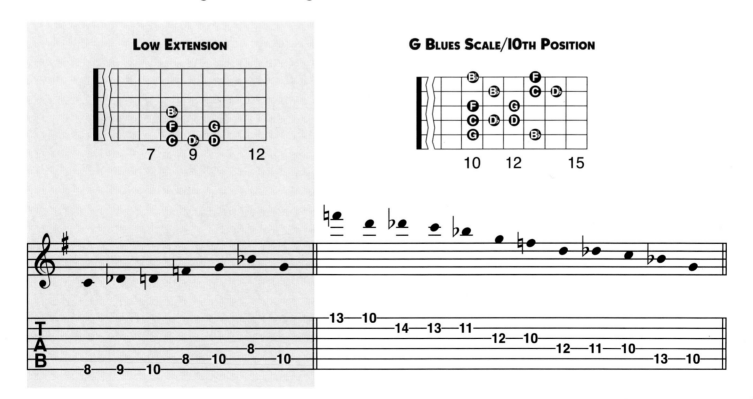

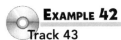

EXAMPLE 42

Track 43

The best way to familiarize yourself with this new layout of notes is to take ideas from the known 3rd position area and transpose or "work them out by ear" in 10th position. The fingerings will differ and the transition may be tricky at first, but keep working on it until both neck positions become comfortable. Here are a couple of examples of this method.

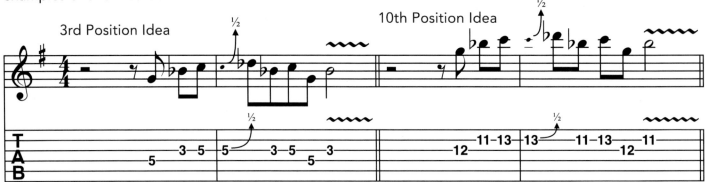

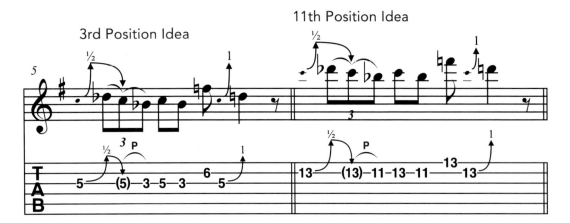

Track 44

SWEET NOTES

The blues scale is the mainstay of blues. It has a serious, dark character. To add contrast or "sweetness" to it, we are going to bring in some new notes. These notes are new to the scale but not to the chord they are drawn from, G6. In order to sound like your melody matches up with the G6 sound, we will be adding the two notes that stand out the most in the G6 chord, the 3rd (B) and the 6th (E).

EXAMPLE 43

Track 45

Here is a classic blues lick that emphasizes the "sweet notes." The 3rd and 6th are circled. A typical blues scale lick follows it so you can compare the sound.

With Sweet Notes   **Typical Blues Lick Without Sweet Notes**

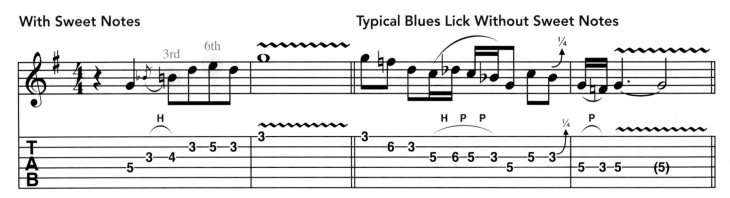

THE B.B. KING SECRET SCALE PATTERN

Now let's check out an area of the neck that blues great B.B. King has spent so much time with, known affectionately by guitar players as "the B.B. box." This is an ideal pattern for soloing because the sweet notes are arranged comfortably under your fingers, while the blues scale notes are never far from reach. Shown here in the key of G, this box pattern is two frets higher than the high blues scale extension.

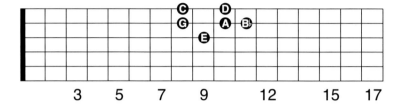

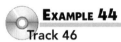

EXAMPLE 44
Track 46

In this example, the sweet notes are circled and identified by interval. Pay attention to the fact that these notes are sometimes played as bends, which emphasizes them musically.

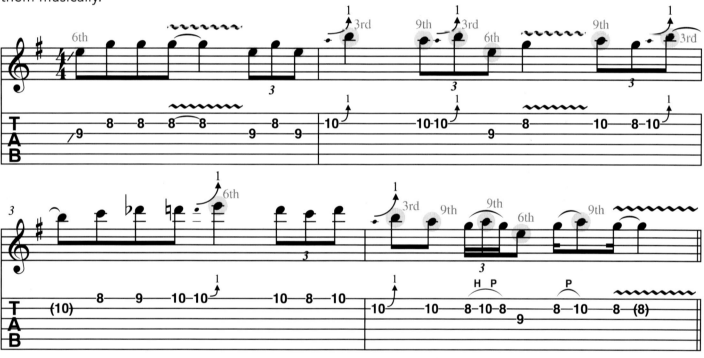

EXAMPLE 45
Track 47

The mark of an experienced bluesman is the ability to mix the moods of the blues scale and the sweet notes to a balancing point. Experiment by starting with one and answering with the other. Here is an example beginning with the blues scale at the high extension and answering with the "sweet spot" position, two frets higher.

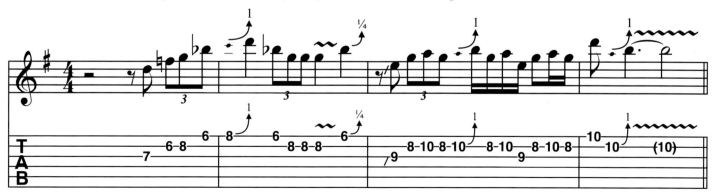

VIBRATO

Vibrato is another very integral mark of musicianship for singers and players of any instrument, and the slow blues offers many opportunities to put it to use. Vibrato takes more time to develop than many other techniques, but it is well worth the time and effort as it is probably the most personal and identifiable part of a guitar player's sound.

Whichever string it is applied to, vibrato is nothing more than a repetitive slight bend played at varying speeds. The high strings (1st–3rd) are generally "pushed" upward (toward the ceiling) when vibrato is applied. The low strings are "pulled" downward (toward the floor). When playing vibrato on bent notes, the string is allowed to fall back down from the destination pitch towards the fretted note—at varying degrees based on vibrato speed and intensity.

Vibrato techniques are extremely difficult to teach and therefore require your utmost attention and concentration. Listen to the vibrato of your favorite guitarists and, most importantly, listen to your own.

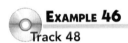
Example 46
Track 48

First let's just add vibrato to the note G on the 2nd string, 8th fret. Use your 3rd finger, reinforced by your 1st and 2nd fingers. Pivot your wrist back and forth to repeatedly bend and return the string. The faster you do this, the more like a natural vibrato it will sound. Strive for control of the width and speed of the vibrato.

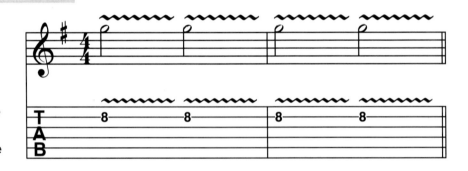

Example 47
Track 49

Adding vibrato to a bent note is more difficult because as you slightly release the bend from its destination pitch, it is essential that you control the return to that pitch accurately—regardless of how wide or fast you choose the vibrato to be.

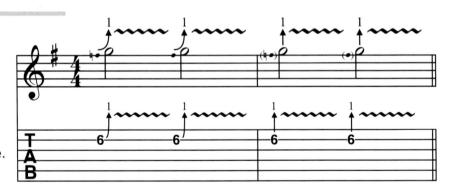

Track 50
Dynamics

Experiment with picking notes as softly as possible—at a whisper level. Also try picking with your fingertips instead of the pick for a rounder tone. Then, without using your volume controls, play as loud as you can. Amplification aside, this is your dynamic range—it's all in your hands. Like with vibrato, strive for dynamic control of your instrument at all times.

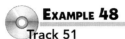

EXAMPLE 48
Track 51

Now we are going to play another call and response over the I chord that brings together all of the blues scale positions and the sweet notes. Take your time with your response and remember the most important point is to get close to the general "vibe" and shape of the lines. You can always go back to the beginning and try to get closer to playing exactly what you hear.

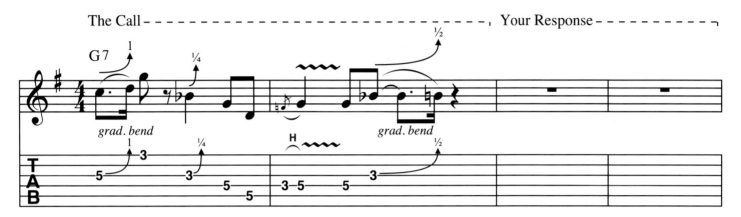

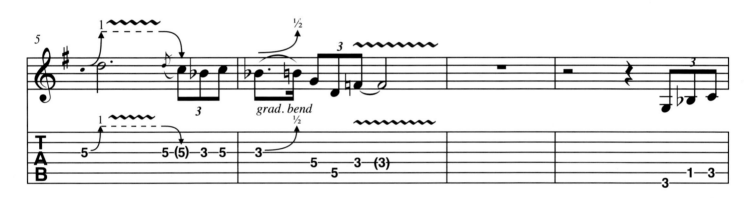

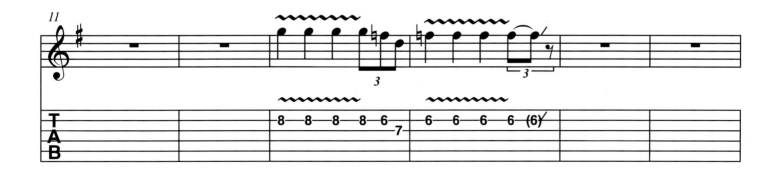

MATCHING SOLOS TO CHORDS

EXAMPLE 49
Track 52

Compare the G6 and C7 (I and IV) chords shown below. The crucial difference is the change from B♮ to B♭. Otherwise the two remaining notes (G and E) are common to both. The solo lick arpeggiates each chord. Practice going back and forth from the I chord to the IV highlighting the change from B♮ to B♭.

EXAMPLE 50
Track 53

Now let's extend this concept to an entire 12-bar blues progression.

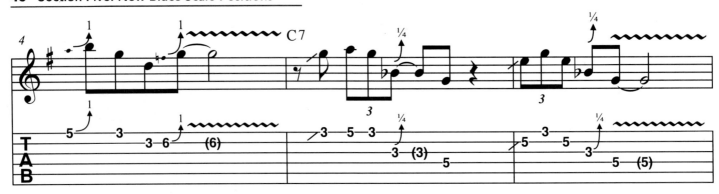

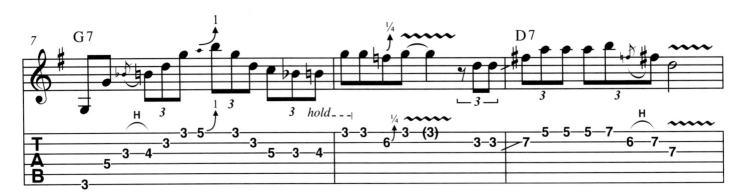

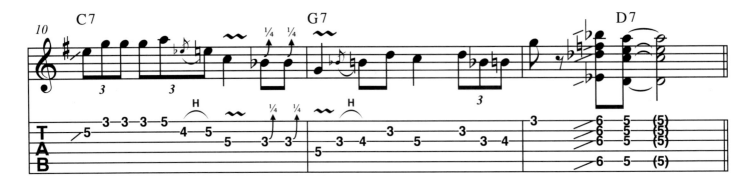

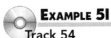 **EXAMPLE 51**

Track 54

Some classic blues licks, like this one in the style of B.B. King, are derived directly from chord shapes. Here, a dominant 7th sound is transposed from the I chord (G7) to the IV (C7) and V (D7) chords.

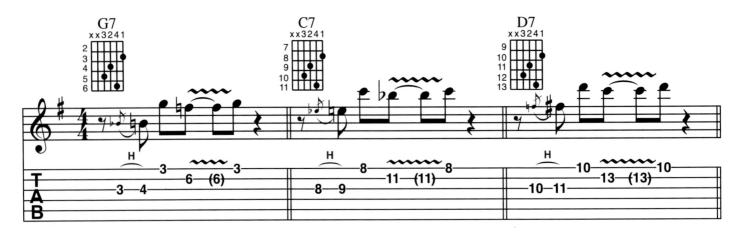

EXAMPLE 52

Track 55

Now let's move all of the patterns to the key of C. Try to work in the same types of parts that we used for the keys of G and A. Remember to think of chord shapes as springboards for matching lead lines to. The 8th position, C Blues Scale (C, E♭, F, F♯, G, B♭) is a good "home base" for all of our fingerings and licks. See below for how the scales and extensions lay out in the key of C.

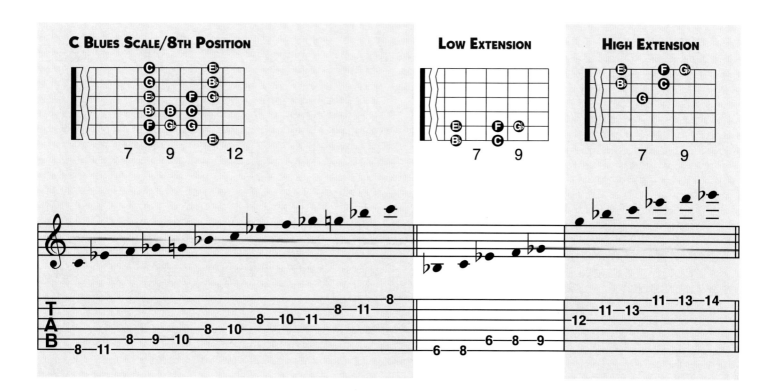

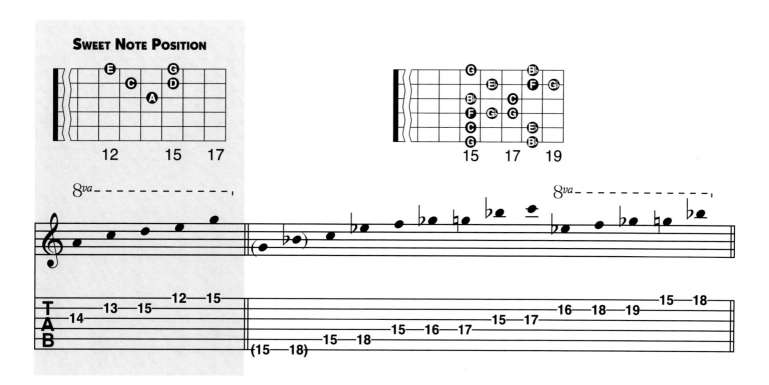

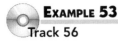

EXAMPLE 53

Track 56

In this solo, pay close attention to the excellent balance between the moods of the blues scale and the sweet notes, the lengths of short and long phrases, and dynamic levels from soft to loud.

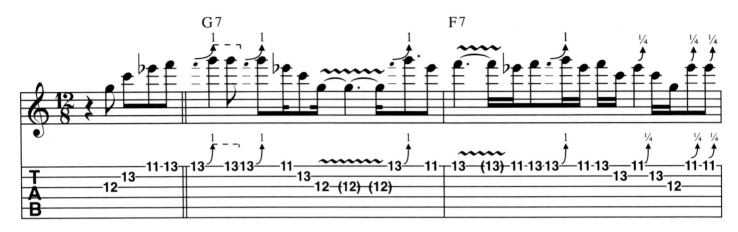

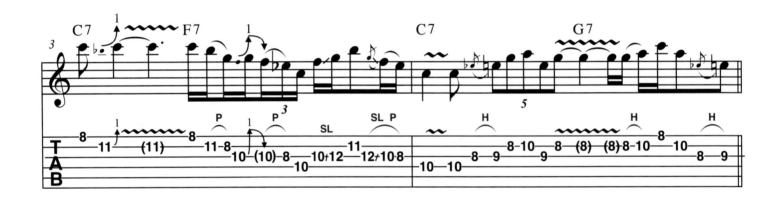

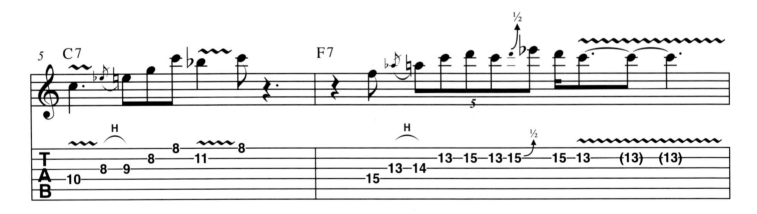

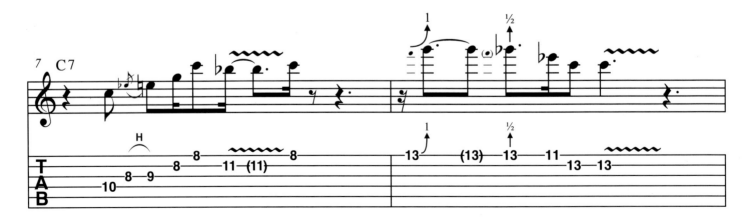

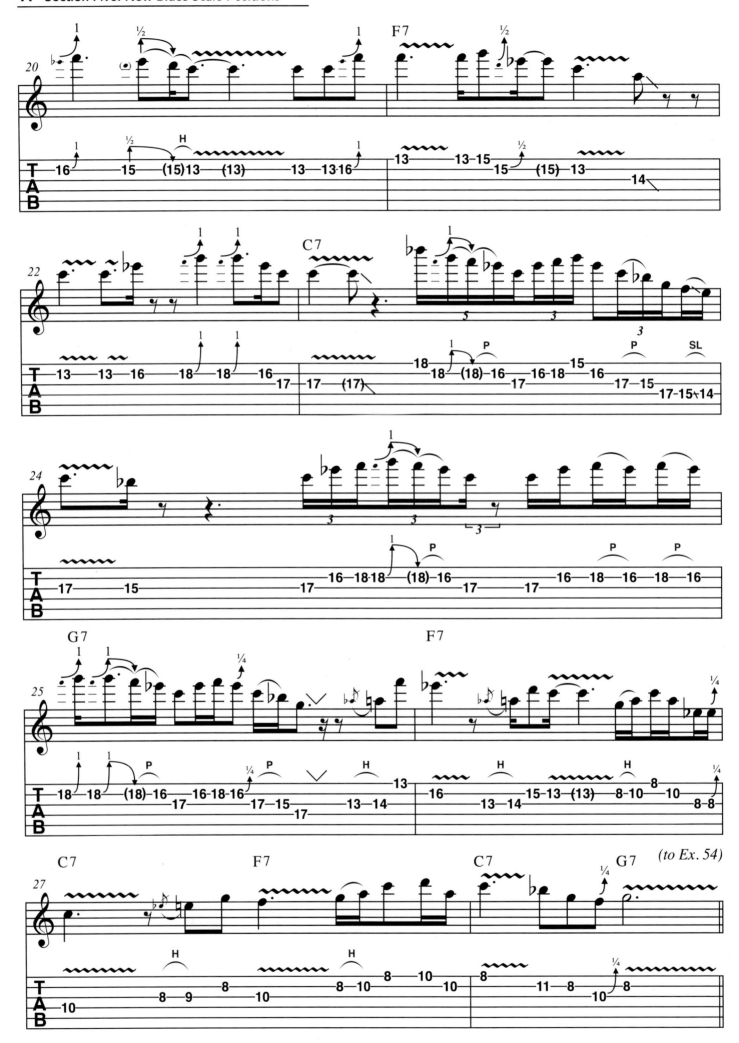

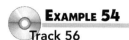

EXAMPLE 54

Track 56

This example is the rhythm guitar part that follows the solo (Example 53) on track 56. Note how these chord voicings were transposed from the other keys and how well-balanced the playing is overall. The mark of an experienced rhythm player is knowing how to become "invisible" by playing the right chords at the right dynamic level consistently through the course of someone's solo. Strive for this by always listening carefully to the soloist and the rhythm section simultaneously.

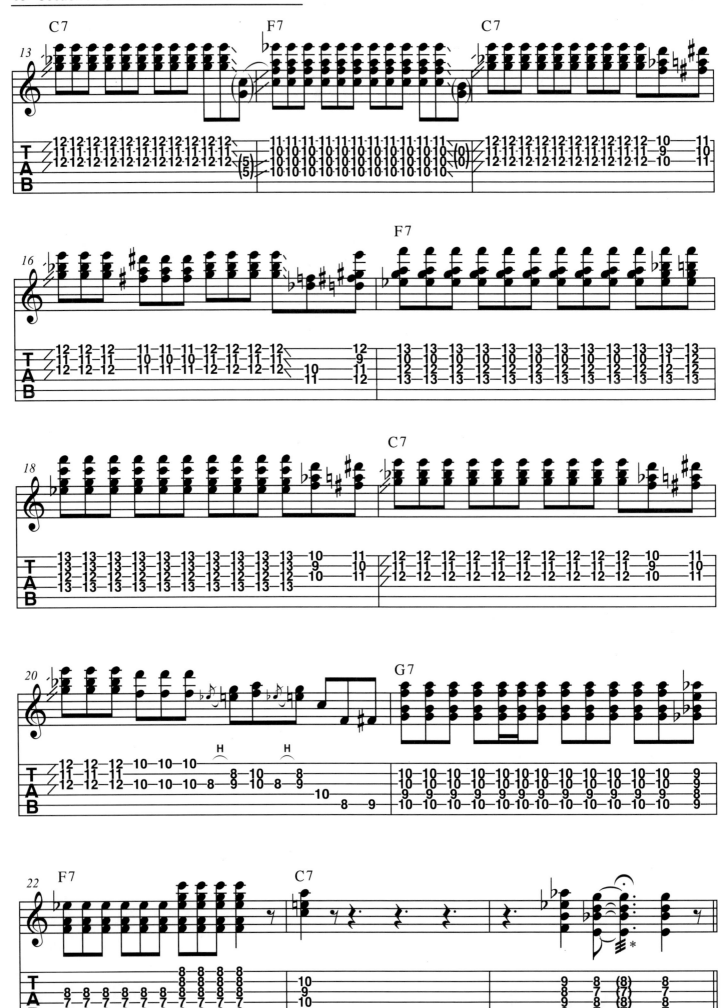

Tremolo. A rapidly repeated note or chord.

Guitar TAB Glossary

TABLATURE EXPLANATION

READING TABLATURE: Tablature illustrates the six strings of the guitar. Notes and chords are indicated by the placement of fret numbers on a given string(s).

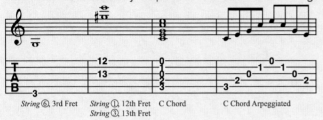

String ⑥, 3rd Fret   String ①, 12th Fret   C Chord   C Chord Arpeggiated
                      String ③, 13th Fret

BENDING NOTES

HALF STEP: Play the note and bend the string one half step.

WHOLE STEP: Play the note and bend the string one whole step.

WHOLE STEP AND A HALF: Play the note and bend the string a whole step and a half.

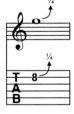

SLIGHT BEND (Microtone): Play the note and bend the string slightly to the equivalent of half a fret.

PREBEND (Ghost Bend): Bend to the specified note, before the string is picked.

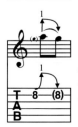

PREBEND AND RELEASE: Bend the string, play it, then release to the original note.

REVERSE BEND: Play the already-bent string, then immediately drop it down to the fretted note.

BEND AND RELEASE: Play the note and gradually bend to the next pitch, then release to the original note. Only the first note is attacked.

UNISON BEND: Play both notes and immediately bend the lower note to the same pitch as the higher note.

DOUBLE NOTE BEND: Play both notes and immediately bend both strings simultaneously.

BENDS INVOLVING MORE THAN ONE STRING: Play the note and bend the string while playing an additional note (or notes) on another string(s). Upon release, relieve pressure from the additional note(s), causing the original note to sound alone.

BENDS INVOLVING STATIONARY NOTES: Play two notes and bend the lower pitch, then hold until the release begins (indicated at the point where the line becomes solid).

TREMOLO BAR

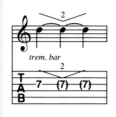

SPECIFIED INTERVAL: The pitch of a note or chord is lowered to a specified interval and then may or may not return to the original pitch. The activity of the tremolo bar is graphically represented by peaks and valleys.

UNSPECIFIED INTERVAL: The pitch of a note or chord is lowered to an unspecified interval.

HARMONICS

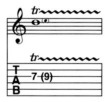

NATURAL HARMONIC: A finger of the fretting hand lightly touches the note or notes indicated in the TAB and is played by the pick hand.

ARTIFICIAL HARMONIC: The first TAB number is fretted, then the picking hand produces the harmonic by using a finger to lightly touch the same string at the second TAB number (in parenthesis) and picking with another finger.

ARTIFICIAL "PINCH" HARMONIC: A note is fretted as indicated by the TAB, then the picking hand produces the harmonic by squeezing the pick firmly while using the tip of the index finger in the pick attack. If parenthesis are found around the fretted note, it does not sound. No parenthesis means both the fretted note and A.H. are heard simultaneously.

RHYTHM SLASHES

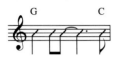 **STRUM INDICATIONS:** Strum with the indicated rhythm. The chord voicings are found on the first page of the transcription underneath the song title.

 **INDICATING SINGLE NOTES USING RHYTHM SLASHES:** Very often single notes are incorporated into a rhythm part. The note name is indicated above the rhythm slash with a fret number and a string indication.

ARTICULATIONS

 **HAMMER-ON:** Play the lower note, then "hammer on" to a higher note with another finger. Only the first note is attacked.

 **LEFT HAND HAMMER:** Hammer on the first note played on each string with the left hand.

 **PULL-OFF:** Play the higher note, then "pull off" to a lower note with another finger. Only the first note is attacked.

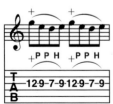 **FRETBOARD TAPPING:** "Tap" onto the note indicated by + with a finger of the picking hand, then pull off to the following note held by the fret hand.

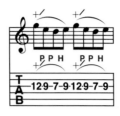 **TAP SLIDE:** Same as fretboard tapping, but the tapped note is slid randomly up the fretboard, then pulled off to the following note.

 **BEND AND TAP TECHNIQUE:** Play a note and bend to the specified interval. While holding the bend, tap onto the note indicated.

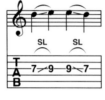 **LEGATO SLIDE:** Play a note and slide to the following note. Only first note is attacked.

 **LONG GLISSANDO:** Play a note and slide in the specified direction for the full value of the note.

 **SHORT GLISSANDO:** Play a note for its full value and slide in the specified direction at the last possible moment.

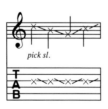 **PICK SLIDE:** Slide the edge of the pick in the specified direction across the length of the string(s).

 **MUTED STRINGS:** A percussive sound is made by laying the fretting hand across all six strings while the picking hand strikes the specified area (low, middle, or high strings).

 **PALM MUTE:** The note or notes are muted by the palm of the picking hand by lightly touching the string(s) near the bridge.

 **TREMOLO PICKING:** The note or notes are picked as fast as possible.

 **TRILL:** Hammer-on and pull-off consecutively and as fast as possible between the original note and the grace note.

 **ACCENT:** Notes or chords are to be played with added emphasis.

 **STACCATO** (Detached Notes): Notes or chords are to be played roughly half their actual value and with separation.

 **DOWNSTROKES AND UPSTROKES:** Notes or chords are to be played with either a downstroke (■) or upstroke (V) of the pick.

 **VIBRATO:** The pitch of a note is varied by a rapid shaking of the fretting hand finger, wrist, and forearm.